# By the same author

## Teaching Python Programming:

An innovative and practical approach

**Practical version**

**20 Concrete examples** (*Programming fundamentals, Control structures, Data collections, Advanced programming, Data structures and algorithms*)

## Les réseaux informatiques: Kit de survie

*Master IP addresses and computer networks in No Time!*

*A Bernard*

# Préface

Computing, by its very nature, is in constant evolution. Yesterday's methods may not be suitable for today's challenges, and educators often find themselves at a crossroads, seeking innovative ways to impart essential skills to a new generation of learners. It is in this context that the idea for this book was conceived.

The origin of this work is based on a simple observation: despite the multitude of resources available, there was a lack of a structured and proven pedagogical approach to teaching programming, especially to those who are taking their first steps. The "Use-Modify-Create" (UMC) approach proved to be this much sought-after method, offering a logical and intuitive progression for learners. But how to implement it effectively? How to adapt it to different teaching contexts? These questions were the starting point of this writing journey.

This book has been designed as a compass for computer science teachers, whether novice or experienced. It aims to provide a clear understanding of the UMC approach, while offering practical advice, concrete examples, and strategies for integrating it into various educational situations. Each chapter has been carefully crafted to guide you step by step, from theory to practice.

Regarding how to approach this book, I advise you to do so with an open and curious mind. Feel free to annotate the margins, highlight passages that speak to you, and revisit certain concepts to delve deeper. Although structured sequentially, each chapter can also be read independently, depending on your needs and interests.

As for the genre of this book, it sits at the crossroads between a pedagogical guide and a reflection on teaching programming. The perspective adopted is that of a fellow traveler, sharing both theoretical knowledge and feedback from experience, with the goal of supporting you in your educational mission.

In conclusion, I hope that this book will be a source of inspiration and a valuable tool in your teaching. May the "Use-Modify-Create" approach open new perspectives for you and accompany you in training the next generation of passionate and competent programmers.

Miguel DELAMONTAGNE

# Summary


Introduction...........................................................................................3
- Presentation of the "Use-Modify-Create" approach...........................3
- Why this book is essential for computer science teachers.................4

Chapter 1: Background and Origins.........................................................5
- History of the UMC approach...........................................................5
- The need for effective pedagogy in computer science.......................8

Chapter 2: Understanding the UMC Approach..........................................10
- "Use" Phase: Introduction and immersion........................................10
- "Modify" Phase: Exploration and adaptation....................................14
- "Create" Phase: Innovation and creation.........................................18

Chapter 3: Benefits of the UMC..............................................................24
- Why choose UMC?..........................................................................24
- Pedagogical and psychological benefits...........................................27
- UMC compared to other teaching methods.......................................31

Chapter 4: Implementing UMC in the classroom........................................35
- Preparation and planning................................................................35
- Does the UMC approach utilize the principles of constructivism?......36
- Can the UMC approach be used in an inductive teaching approach?39
- Can the UMC approach be used as a "trigger" activity in a sequence?
...........................................................................................................42
- Can the UMC approach be used in a revision activity?......................45

Chapter 5: Feedback and reflection.........................................................48
- Introduction....................................................................................48
- Challenges and problems encountered.............................................50
- Educationnal objectives...................................................................56
- Why use the UMC approach?...........................................................59
- Advantages and disadvantages.......................................................63

Conclusion...........................................................................................65
- The future of UMC in computer science education.............................65
- Encouraging a culture of continuous learning Appendices................66

Glossary of terms.................................................................................67

# Introduction

## Presentation of the "Use-Modify-Create" approach

Computing, while technical on the surface, is deeply rooted in creativity and innovation. Yet, how can one introduce novices to this vast field in a structured manner while preserving the spirit of innovation? This is where the "Use-Modify-Create" (UMC) approach comes into play. In this section, we will introduce UMC, a pedagogical method that proposes a logical and intuitive progression for learning programming and computational thinking. We will explore its origins, fundamental principles, and how it structures the learning of programming in a way that fosters both understanding and creativity.

## Why is this book essential for computer science teachers?

Teaching computer science is a unique challenge. Unlike other disciplines, it must constantly evolve and adapt to a rapidly changing technological landscape. Moreover, it needs to balance the teaching of technical skills with the development of critical and creative thinking. In this section, we will discuss the complexity of teaching computer science in the modern era and the necessity of adopting solid and proven pedagogical methods. We will highlight why UMC, as an approach, meets these challenges and why this book, as a guide, is an indispensable tool for any computer science teacher looking to provide quality education while inspiring the next generation of digital thinkers and creators.

# Chapter 1: Context and origins

## History of the UMC approach

The history of the "Use-Modify-Create" (UMC) approach is deeply rooted in the ongoing quest to improve teaching and learning in computer science. As technology and programming became increasingly central in our modern world, it became imperative to find teaching methods that not only transmit technical skills, but also cultivate critical and creative thinking.

**Teaching methods in computer science**

Prior to the advent of the UMC approach, several methods were used to teach programming and computer thinking. Among these, the traditional approach based on lectures, where students were primarily passive receivers of information. Although this method had its utility, it did not necessarily promote active engagement or creativity in students.

**Gaps and challenges**

Over time, educators realized that many students struggled to apply concepts learned passively to real-world situations. Moreover, student motivation often decreased when faced with purely theoretical tasks. It became clear that a new approach was needed, one that would place students at the center of their learning.

---

**Birth of UMC**

In this context, the UMC (Use-Modify-Create) approach was born. Inspired by active and student-centered teaching methods, UMC was designed to address the specific challenges of teaching programming. It encourages students to interact directly with the code, modify it according to their needs, and ultimately, create their own solutions.

---

**Pioneers and key thinkers**

Although the term and concept of UMC (Use-Modify-Create) are relatively recent, its fundamental principles have been influenced by educators and theorists such as Jean Piaget, with his theory of knowledge construction, and Seymour Papert, who promoted the idea that children learn best by doing.

---

**Early implementations**

The first implementations of the UMC (Use-Modify-Create) approach were observed in workshops and coding camps for children, where educators noticed the benefits of this method in terms of engagement and understanding. Since then, UMC has been adopted in a wide range of educational settings, from primary schools to universities, demonstrating its versatility and effectiveness.

In conclusion, the "Use-Modify-Create" approach is the result of a constant evolution in computer science pedagogy, aiming to meet the changing needs of students and to prepare the next generation of competent and creative computer thinkers.

# The Need for effective computer science pedagogy

Computer science, although often perceived as a mere series of codes and algorithms, is in fact a deeply interdisciplinary discipline that encompasses logic, creativity, problem-solving, and much more. Its teaching requires an approach that goes beyond the simple transmission of technical knowledge.

**Unique challenges of teaching computer science**

Computer science is a constantly evolving discipline. Languages, tools, and technologies change rapidly, sometimes rendering skills learned in just a few years obsolete. Moreover, unlike other subjects, computer science requires abstract thinking and the ability to visualize processes that are invisible to the naked eye. These characteristics present unique challenges in teaching and learning.

**Common obstacles for teachers**

Many teachers, even those with a strong background in computer science, encounter obstacles when it comes to imparting their knowledge. Some of these challenges include combating preconceived notions of students, managing the diversity of skills in a classroom, and finding a balance between theory and practical application. Additionally, student motivation can fluctuate, especially when they are faced with difficult concepts or repeated errors.

**Why a strong pedagogy is crucial?**

In the digital age, proficiency in computer science has become as fundamental as reading, writing, and mathematics. It opens doors to promising careers, stimulates innovation, and is essential for understanding the world around us. However, without effective pedagogy, students risk disengagement, developing gaps in their knowledge, or lacking confidence in their skills.

**Failures of traditional methods**

Traditional teaching methods, often based on lectures and repetitive exercises, do not always meet the needs of computer science students. These methods may lack interactivity, not encourage critical thinking, or fail to allow students to apply what they have learned in a practical manner.

**UMC: A response to the Need**

In response to these challenges, the "Use-Modify-Create" approach has emerged as a promising solution.

It recognizes that learning is an active process and that students learn best by doing. UMC provides a clear structure, allowing students to progress gradually, while giving them the necessary space to explore, experiment, and innovate.

In summary, teaching computer science requires a thoughtful consideration of how concepts are presented and assimilated. The "Use-Modify-Create" approach provides a suitable response to this need, placing the student at the center of their learning and promoting a deep and lasting understanding of the discipline.

# Chapter 2:
# Understanding the UMC approach

## "Use" Phase: Introduction and immersion

*The first step of UMC is essential to establish a solid foundation. In this section, we will explore in depth the "Use" phase. We will discuss its importance as an entry point for novices, how it allows students to familiarize themselves with new concepts and tools, and strategies for effectively implementing it in the classroom. We will also examine concrete examples of activities and projects that correspond to this phase, offering teachers practical ideas for their own curriculum.*

The "Use" phase is the first step of the "Use-Modify-Create" (UMC) approach and serves as a springboard for the subsequent stages. It plays a crucial role in introducing students to programming and computational thinking.

**Importance as an entry point for novices**

For many students, programming can seem intimidating. The 'Use' phase offers a gentle introduction, allowing students to engage with pre-existing code without the pressure of having to create it themselves. By working with concrete examples, students can quickly see the results of their work, which boosts their confidence and interest in the subject.

**Getting familiar with new concepts and tools**

Before being able to modify or create code, students must first understand the basics. The 'Use' phase allows them to become familiar with fundamental programming concepts such as loops, variables, and functions, as well as with tools and development environments. By interacting with existing code, they can see these concepts in action, which makes understanding them easier.

**Strategies for effective implementation in the classroom**

To maximize the effectiveness of the 'Use' phase, teachers can adopt several strategies:

- **Start with simple examples**: Begin with short and simple codes to avoid overwhelming the students.

- **Encourage exploration**: Allow students to play with the code, test it, and see how it responds to different modifications.

- **Class discussion**: After working with an example, organize a class discussion to break down the code and clarify the concepts.

---

**Concrete examples of activities and projects**

Here are some activity ideas that correspond to the 'Use' phase:

- **Program analysis**: Provide students with a small program and ask them to predict what it will do before running it.

- **Minor modification**: After introducing an example, ask students to make small changes, such as changing the values of variables or the order of instructions.

- **Code-Based Games**: Use educational games where students can interact with pre-existing code to achieve a specific objective.

In conclusion, the 'Use' phase is an essential step in the UMC that prepares the ground for subsequent phases. By offering an accessible and engaging introduction to programming, it lays the foundation for successful learning.

# Modify Phase: Exploration and Adaptation

*After laying the foundations, it's time to delve deeper. The 'Modify' phase encourages students to take what they have learned and adapt it to their own needs or interests. In this section, we'll discuss the goals of this phase, how it promotes critical thinking, and how it prepares students to become active creators. We'll also share examples of activities and challenges that encourage modifications, as well as tips for guiding students through this exploratory process.*

The 'Modify' phase is a crucial intermediate step in the 'Use-Modify-Create' (UMC) approach. It serves as a bridge between the passive use of pre-existing codes and the active creation of original solutions. This phase is essential for developing students' autonomy, creativity, and critical thinking.

**Goals of the 'Modify' Phase**

The main goal of this phase is to enable students to take ownership of the knowledge they have acquired. By modifying existing code, they are led to:

- Understand the workings of the code in depth.
- Experiment and test different solutions.
- Learn through trial and error.

**Promoting critical thinking**

Active code modification encourages students to ask questions, identify problems, and think about solutions. Rather than simply accepting the code as it is, they are encouraged to wonder, 'Why does it work this way?' or 'How could I make it better or different?'. This approach strengthens their ability to analyze and critically evaluate code.

**Preparation for becoming active creators**

By modifying code, students begin to see the infinite possibilities of programming. They learn that code is not fixed but can be adapted and transformed to meet various needs and objectives. This realization is essential to prepare them for the 'Create' phase, where they will develop their own solutions from scratch.

**Examples of activities and challenges**

Here are some ideas to encourage students to modify code:

- **Modification challenges**: Provide a base code and set specific challenges, such as 'Modify this game to add a new level' or 'Adapt this program to work with different types of data'.

- **Bug analysis**: Provide a code with intentional errors and ask students to identify and correct them.

- **Project extensions**: After working on a project during the 'Use' phase, ask students to extend or improve it in some way.

**Tips for guiding students**

During the 'Modify' phase, it's essential to provide appropriate support and guidance. Here are some tips for teachers:

- **Encourage experimentation**: Remind students that it's okay to make mistakes and that they can learn from them.

- **Ask open-ended questions**: Rather than giving answers, ask questions that guide the students' thinking.

- **Provide resources**: Offer examples, tutorials, or references that can help students when they are stuck.

In conclusion, the 'Modify' phase is a vital step in transforming students from mere code consumers into active creators. It offers a unique opportunity for exploration, adaptation, and growth, thereby laying the groundwork for the final phase of creation.

# Create phase: Innovation and creation

*The final phase of the UMC is where the real magic happens. In this section, we will explore the 'Create' phase in detail, discussing its importance for student autonomy, how it encourages innovation, and the satisfaction it brings in allowing students to realize their own projects. We will examine best practices for supporting students in this phase, examples of successful projects, and strategies for meaningfully assessing student work.*

The 'Create' phase is the culmination of the 'Use-Modify-Create' (UMC) approach. This is the stage where students are encouraged to apply everything they have learned and create something entirely new. This phase is crucial for developing students' creativity, innovation, and autonomy.

**Importance for student autonomy**

The 'Create' phase gives students the freedom to make their own decisions, choose their projects, and determine how to accomplish them. This autonomy strengthens their confidence and allows them to take initiatives. They are no longer just consumers of content but become active creators.

**Encouraging innovation**

With the freedom to create, students are encouraged to innovate. They can explore new ideas, experiment with different concepts, and find unique solutions to problems. This phase cultivates an innovator's mindset, where students are encouraged to think outside the box.

**Satisfaction of realizing one's own projects**

There is immense satisfaction in seeing an idea turn into reality. The 'Create' phase offers students the opportunity to experience this. After working hard, overcoming challenges, and learning new concepts, they can see the fruits of their efforts in the form of a completed project

**Best practices to support students**

Here are some tips for teachers to effectively support their students during the 'Create' phase:

- **Provide resources**: Ensure that students have access to resources, tutorials, and examples to assist them in their projects.

- **Encourage collaboration**: Promoting teamwork and collaboration can help students share ideas and solve problems together.

- **Offer constructive feedback**: Instead of just assessing, provide feedback that helps students improve their work.

**Examples of successful projects**

Projects such as creating an app, designing a website, developing a video game, or programming a robot are examples of what students can accomplish during this phase.

**Assessment strategies**

Assessing students' work during the 'Create' phase should go beyond just checking the correctness of the code. Consider instead:

- The creativity and originality of the project.
- The complexity and depth of thinking.
- The ability to solve problems and overcome challenges.

In conclusion, the 'Create' phase is an essential step in the UMC that allows students to fully realize their potential as creators and innovators. It offers a unique opportunity for learning, growth, and personal expression.

# Summary :

The 'Use-Modify-Create' (UMC) approach is an educational method used to teach computational thinking and programming. It is designed to help students progressively advance in their understanding and mastery of computer concepts. Here's how it works:

1. **Use** In this first step, students are exposed to existing code or a program. They use it to understand how it works without necessarily modifying it. This allows them to become familiar with the code and to see how it functions in a given context.

2. **Modify** Once students have a basic understanding of the code, they are encouraged to modify it to do something slightly different or to meet a new set of requirements. This helps them develop a deeper understanding of the code and learn how to make changes without breaking everything.

3. **Create**    In this final step, students are encouraged to create their own code from scratch, using the knowledge and skills they have acquired in the first two steps. This gives them the opportunity to put into practice everything they have learned and to create something entirely new.

The UMC approach is beneficial because it offers a natural progression from familiarization to creation, allowing students to build their confidence and competence at each stage. It also encourages students to develop an increasing sense of ownership over the code they write, which can motivate them to continue learning and creating.

# Chapter 3: Advantages of the UMC

## Why choose UMC?

Computer science education is rapidly evolving, with new challenges and opportunities constantly emerging. In this changing context, the "Use-Modify-Create" (UMC) approach stands out as a solid and effective pedagogical method. Here's why it deserves special attention.

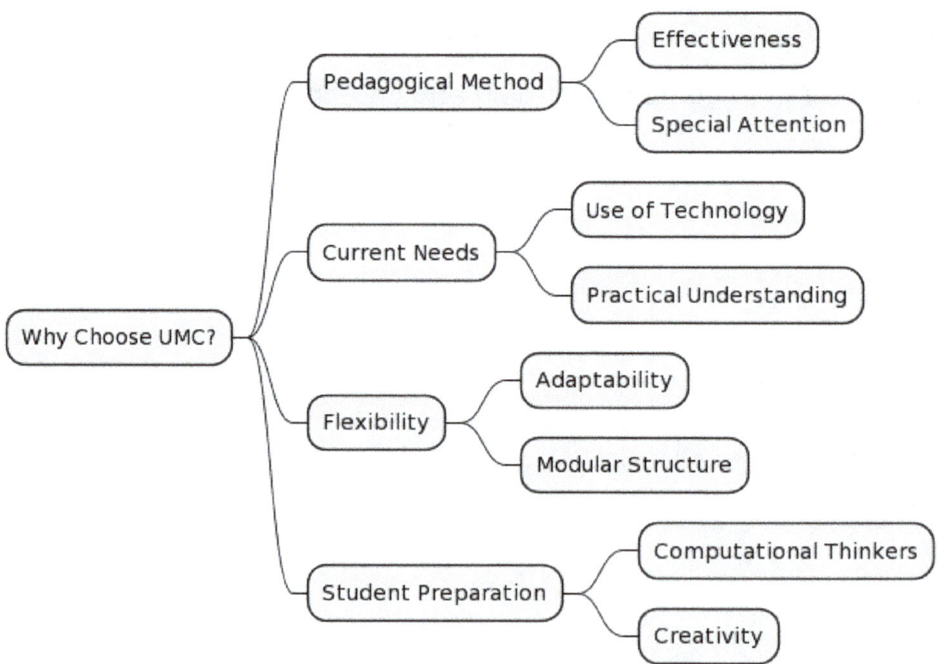

**Meeting current needs in computer science education**

With the rapid expansion of technology in almost every aspect of our daily lives, it is imperative that students not only understand how to use technology but also how it works. The UMC offers a logical progression that begins with using pre-existing tools and code, allowing students to familiarize themselves with concepts before modifying them and, ultimately, creating their own solutions. This progression ensures that students acquire a deep and practical understanding of computer science.

**Flexibility for different teaching contexts**

Whether you are teaching in a large university, a small high school, or even in an informal setting like an after-school workshop, the UMC is flexible enough to adapt to different contexts. Its modular structure allows teachers to adapt it based on available time, resources, and the skill level of the students.

**Effective preparation of students**

The UMC does not just transmit technical skills; it aims to develop competent computer thinkers. Students learn to approach problems systematically, think critically, and be creative in their solutions. By going through the "Use", "Modify", and "Create" phases, they are exposed to a full range of learning experiences, from the basics to independent creation. This prepares them not only for more advanced studies in computer science but also to navigate an increasingly digital world.

Choosing a pedagogical approach for teaching computer science is an important decision that can have long-lasting impacts on student success. The "Use-Modify-Create" approach offers a proven and flexible method that meets the current needs of computer science education. It effectively prepares students to become not only competent users of technology but also creators and innovators. For these reasons and many more, UMC deserves to be seriously considered by all computer science educators.

# Pedagogical and Psychological Benefits

The "Use-Modify-Create" (UMC) approach does not merely provide a framework for learning programming; it encompasses a teaching philosophy aimed at enriching the educational experience of students on multiple levels.

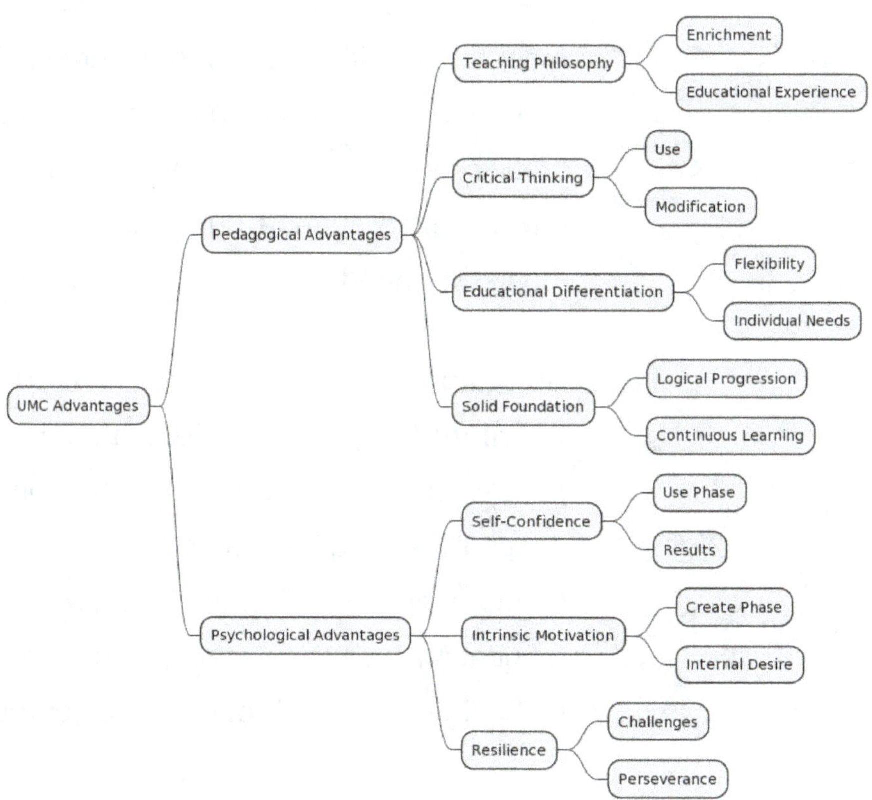

**Pedagogical benefits**

**Promotion of critical thinking:** The UMC encourages students not to simply accept information as it is presented. By starting with using existing codes or programs and then modifying them, students are led to critically reflect on the internal workings and underlying logics.

1. **Facilitation of educational differentiation**: The UMC is flexible and can be adapted to meet the individual needs of students. Teachers can offer additional challenges during the modification phase for advanced students, or provide extra support during the use phase for those who need it.

2. **Building a solid foundation for continuous learning**: By guiding students through a logical progression, the UMC ensures that fundamental concepts are well understood before moving on to more advanced skills. This creates a solid foundation on which students can continue to build throughout their educational journey.

**Psychological**

**Increase in self-confidence**: Starting with the "Use"

**Benefits**    phase, where students can quickly see results and succeed, they develop confidence in their ability to tackle more complex tasks. This confidence is reinforced at each step, culminating in the "Create" phase where they can take pride in their own creations.

1. **Intrinsic motivation:** The UMC offers students the opportunity to work on projects that are meaningful to them, especially during the "Create" phase. This can lead to intrinsic motivation, where students are driven by an internal desire to learn and create, rather than by external rewards.

2. **Development of resilience in facing challenges**: Programming is inherently filled with challenges and errors. The UMC, by guiding students through these challenges in a structured way, helps them develop resilience and perseverance in the face of adversity.

In summary, the "Use-Modify-Create" approach offers much more than just technical skills. It aims to develop the whole person, strengthening both cognitive skills and essential character traits for success in the modern world.

# UMC versus other teaching methods

In the dynamic world of computer science education, teachers often encounter a variety of pedagogical methods, each promising optimal results. The "Use-Modify-Create" (UMC) approach is one of these methods, but how does it stand out from the rest? To answer this question, we first need to examine the distinctive features of UMC and compare them to other popular approaches.

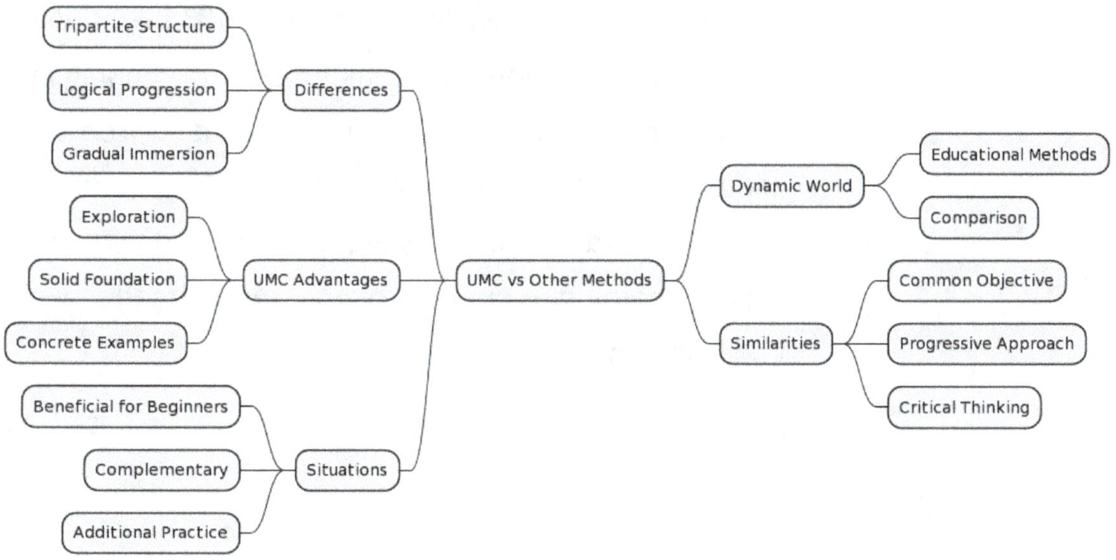

**Similarities with other methods**

Many pedagogical methods in computer science share a common goal: to make the learning of programming and computational thinking accessible and engaging. Like UMC, other methods may also adopt a progressive approach, starting with basic concepts and progressing to more advanced skills. Additionally, there is often a focus on problem-solving, creativity, and critical thinking.

**Key differences**

Where UMC stands out is in its clearly defined tripartite structure. While other methods might dive directly into creation or focus mainly on modifying existing codes, UMC offers a logical progression that guides students through each step. This structure allows for gradual immersion, thereby reducing the steep learning curve often associated with programming.

**Unique advantages of UMC**

One of the main benefits of UMC is that it provides students an opportunity to explore and understand before engaging in creation. This builds confidence and ensures that students have a solid foundation on which to build. Moreover, by focusing first on using and modifying, students are able to see concrete examples and understand practical applications before embarking on their own projects.

**Situations where UMC is preferred or complementary**

UMC is particularly beneficial for beginners or those who may be intimidated by the prospect of programming. However, it can also be used in complement to other methods. For example, a teacher might use a project-based approach for a particular concept, then integrate UMC to reinforce that concept and offer additional practice.

In conclusion, while UMC shares some similarities with other computer science teaching methods, it offers a unique structure and benefits that make it particularly effective for learning programming. Teachers looking to offer a holistic and engaging learning experience would do well to consider UMC as a valuable option in their pedagogical arsenal.

# Chapter 4: Implementing UMC in the classroom

The effectiveness of the "Use-Modify-Create" (UMC) approach lies not only in its structure but also in how it is implemented in the classroom. In this chapter, we will explore the key steps for integrating UMC in computer science teaching, providing practical advice, examples of activities, and strategies for managing the diversity of students' skills.

## Preparation and planning

**Learning objectives**
Before starting, it is essential to clearly define the learning objectives. What are the key concepts that students need to master by the end of the lesson or unit?

**Selection of resources:**
Choose tools, software, and resources that are age-appropriate and skill-level appropriate for the students, and that support the objectives of UMC.

**Planning activities:**
Organize activities in a way that they follow a logical progression, starting with the "Use" phase, then moving to "Modify", and finally to "Create".

## Does the UMC approach use the principles of constructivism?

The "Use-Modify-Create" (UMC) approach aligns with the educational current of constructivism. Constructivism is a learning theory suggesting that individuals actively construct their own understanding and knowledge of the world through their experiences and by reflecting on those experiences.

Here is how UMC aligns with the principles of constructivism:

**Active learning**

In the "Use" phase, students actively interact with pre-existing material, allowing them to familiarize themselves with new concepts without being overwhelmed. This corresponds to the constructivist idea that learning is most effective when the student is actively engaged.

| **Progressive construction of knowledge** | UMC proposes a natural progression from using existing materials to modifying, and then to creating new materials. This reflects the constructivist idea that knowledge is built progressively, building on pre-existing knowledge and skills. |
| --- | --- |
| **Reflection and adaptation** | In the "Modify" phase, students are encouraged to reflect on what they have learned and adapt it to new situations. This aligns with the constructivist principle that reflection on experience is essential for knowledge construction. |
| **Creation and application** | In the "Create" phase, students apply what they have learned to create something new. This corresponds to the constructivist idea that learning is reinforced when students have the opportunity to apply their knowledge in real situations. |

In summary, although the "Use-Modify-Create" approach is not explicitly labeled as constructivist, its principles and structure closely align with the central ideas of constructivism in learning and teaching.

# Can the UMC approach be used in an inductive teaching method?

The "Use-Modify-Create" (UMC) approach fits well within an inductive teaching method. To understand how, let's first define what an inductive approach is.

**Inductive teaching method**

In this approach, learning begins with the observation or experimentation of concrete examples or real-life situations. From these observations, students deduce principles, rules, or theories. In other words, it starts from specific instances and moves towards generalizations.

Here is how UMC aligns with an inductive approach:

**Observation and experimentation**

**Use**: In this phase, students are exposed to concrete examples (codes, scripts, projects, etc.). They use and observe them in action. This corresponds to the first step of the inductive approach where students begin with concrete observations.

**Analysis and exploration**

**Modify**: After using and observing concrete examples, students are encouraged to modify them. In doing so, they begin to analyze how things work and explore the underlying mechanisms. This is an intermediate step between pure observation and the deduction of general principles.

**Deduction and application**

**Create**: In this phase, students apply what they have learned from the first two steps to create something new. This requires a deeper understanding and the ability to deduce general principles from the acquired knowledge. This is the final step of the inductive approach where students move from specific instances to generalizations.

In conclusion, the "Use-Modify-Create" approach naturally aligns with the inductive teaching method. It guides students through a learning process where they start with concrete observations, explore and analyze these observations, and then deduce and apply general principles. This is an effective method for promoting a deep and lasting understanding of the concepts taught.

# Can the UMC approach be used as a "Trigger" activity for a learning sequence?

The "Use-Modify-Create" (UMC) approach can be used as part of a "trigger" activity in a teaching sequence. A trigger activity is designed to spark students' interest, awaken their curiosity, and prepare them to approach a new topic or learning unit. It often serves as an introduction to a teaching sequence.

Here's how UMC can be integrated into a trigger activity:

**Stimulation and discovery - Use**

The trigger activity could start with the "Use" phase of UMC. Present students with a pre-existing tool, application, game, or code related to the subject being studied. Let them use and interact with it. This direct interaction with a concrete element piques their interest and gives them an insight into what they will be learning.

**Questioning and reflection - Modify**

After using the tool or code, ask questions to prompt students to reflect on what they observed. For example, "What would happen if...?" or "How could you change this to achieve a different result?". Encourage them to consider modifications, even if they don't implement them yet. This stimulates their critical thinking and prepares them for the upcoming learning phase.

**Anticipation and projection - Create**

Although the "Create" phase is typically the final step of UMC, in the context of a trigger activity, it can be used to encourage students to anticipate what they might create or accomplish at the end of the teaching sequence. Ask questions like, "What would you like to create based on what you've seen?" or "How could you use what you're going to learn to create something new?".

By integrating UMC into a trigger activity, you can not only capture the students' attention from the beginning of the sequence but also actively prepare them for the upcoming learning. This approach engages them from the start, making them more receptive and enthusiastic about exploring the topic in depth.

# Can the UMC approach be used in a revision activity?

The "Use-Modify-Create" (UMC) approach is quite suitable for revising Python language concepts for students who have already been exposed to these concepts in their first year of study. Here's why this method is particularly effective:

**Reactivation of prior knowledge**

**Use**: This phase allows students to recall and reactivate the knowledge acquired in their first year. By using existing code examples, they can quickly get back into the swing of things and remember key concepts.

**Deepening and understanding**

**Modify**: By modifying existing code, students have the opportunity to deepen their understanding of the concepts. This step encourages exploration and a detailed understanding of the intricacies and nuances of the Python language.

| **Development of advanced skills** | **Create**: This phase challenges students to apply their knowledge in a creative and autonomous way. They can design and develop their own projects, which is essential to prepare them for the demands of their final year and beyond. |
|---|---|
| **Adaptability to individual needs** | UMC allows for the adaptation of activities to the individual needs of students. Those who need more time to catch up can focus more on the "Use" and "Modify" phases, while those who are already comfortable can quickly move on to creative projects. |
| **Encouragement of active learning** | The UMC approach promotes active and engaging learning, which is crucial for maintaining the interest and motivation of students, especially when revising concepts that have already been taught. |
| **Preparation for complex projects** | Students are often faced with more complex and integrated projects. The UMC approach prepares them for this complexity by allowing them to progressively build their programming skills. |

In summary, UMC is a highly suitable pedagogical method for revising and deepening Python concepts in senior computer science classes. It offers a flexible and progressive structure that meets the varied needs of students, while effectively preparing them for the advanced challenges of programming.

# Chapter 5: Experience feedback and reflection

## Introduction

This chapter is a dedicated space for reflection and sharing of lived experiences. The objective of this chapter is twofold. On one hand, it aims to provide an intimate and authentic overview of the challenges and triumphs I have encountered as a computer science teacher, and on the other hand, it aspires to enlighten readers on the reasons that led me to adopt the "Use-Modify-Create" (UMC) approach in my pedagogy.

The importance of this chapter lies in its ability to humanize theory, to highlight the practical realities of teaching computer science, and to demonstrate how UMC can be a tangible response to the problems encountered. It is a testimony from the field, an exploration of motivations, objectives, and outcomes achieved through UMC, all enriched with personal reflections and practical advice.

Throughout this chapter, you will not only discover the behind-the-scenes of implementing the Use-Modify-Create (UMC) approach but also the reasoning, adjustments, and lessons that stem from it. My hope is that this introspection serves as a source of inspiration, encouragement, and guidance for all computer science teachers looking to enrich their practice and optimize their students' learning.

In summary, this chapter is an invitation to discovery, exchange, and reflection on the art of teaching computer science through the prism of the "Use-Modify-Create" approach. May you find in it useful insights, innovative ideas, and perhaps even, a resonance with your own pedagogical experiences and aspirations.

# Challenges and problems encountered

As a computer science teacher, I have faced a multitude of challenges and problems that have shaped my pedagogical journey and influenced my pursuit of effective teaching methods. These challenges, far from being insurmountable obstacles, have been catalysts for growth and opportunities for reflection and improvement.

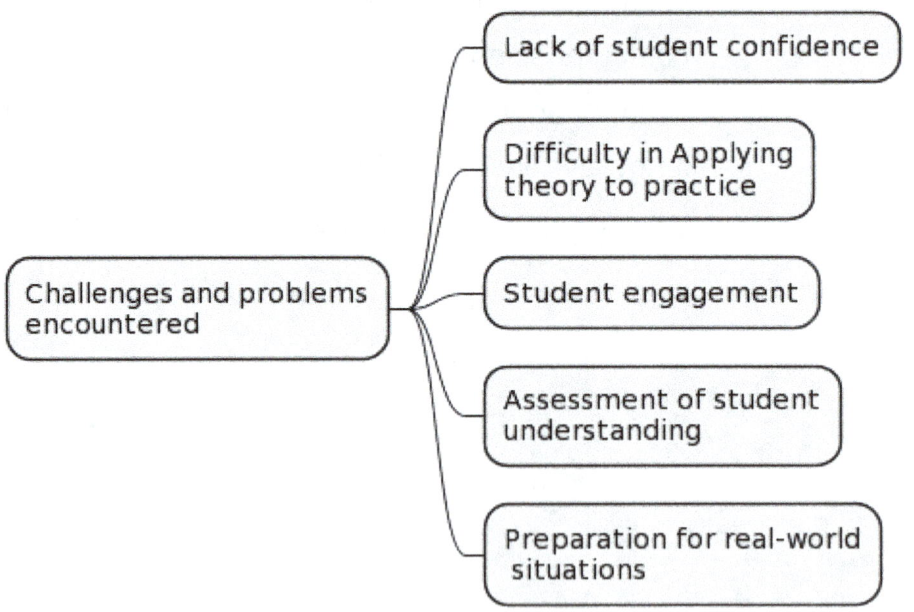

| Heterogeneity of skills | | |
|---|---|---|
| | **Problem** | In a classroom, the diversity of skills is often marked. Some students may have prior experience in programming, while others are new to the discipline. |
| | **Response UMC** | The Use-Modify-Create (UMC) approach, with its progressive nature, provides a common starting point for all students with the "Use" phase. This initial step allows everyone to immerse themselves in the field at their own pace, ensuring a harmonious progression tailored to each individual's skills. |

| **Lack of student confidence** | | |
|---|---|---|
| | **Problem** | Programming can intimidate many students, who doubt their abilities or perceive the discipline as excessively complex. |
| | **Response UMC** | The "Use" phase of the Use-Modify-Create (UMC) approach, by allowing students to work with pre-existing code, provides a reassuring introduction. It serves as a springboard to bolster students' confidence before moving them towards more demanding tasks. |

| **Difficulty in applying theory to practice** | | |
|---|---|---|
| | **Problem** | Students may master theoretical concepts but encounter difficulties in applying them in practical contexts. |
| | **Response UMC** | The Use-Modify-Create (UMC) approach promotes the concrete application of knowledge right from the early stages. The "Modify" and |

| | | |
|---|---|---|
| | | "Create" steps are particularly conducive to establishing links between theory and practice, thus facilitating the integration of concepts. |

**Student engagement**

| | |
|---|---|
| **Problem** | Maintaining student engagement and motivation often proves complex, especially in technical subjects such as programming. |
| **Response UMC** | The Use-Modify-Create (UMC) approach, with its interactive and involving nature, stimulates student engagement. The successive phases of use, modification, and creation maintain interest and encourage active participation. |

| Assessment of student understanding | | |
|---|---|---|
| | **Problem** | Assessing the actual understanding and skills acquired by students is a constant challenge for teachers. |
| | **Response UMC** | Observing students during the code modification and creation phases provides teachers with valuable indicators of each student's level of understanding and the skills they have developed. |

| Preparation for real-world situations | | |
|---|---|---|
| | **Problem** | Students must be equipped to face real professional situations, where they will be required to work on existing code or develop their own solutions. |
| | **Response UMC** | By simulating these scenarios, the Use-Modify-Create (UMC) approach effectively prepares students to navigate the professional world, familiarizing them with concrete and varied situations. |

In conclusion, the "Use-Modify-Create" approach proves to be a robust pedagogical tool in the face of numerous challenges in teaching programming and computational thinking. It offers a clear structure, reinforces student confidence, and promotes a deep understanding of concepts.

# Educational objectives

My educational objectives have always been guided by the desire to provide a stimulating and inclusive learning environment, where each student can explore, understand, and apply computer science concepts in a meaningful way. Here are some of the specific goals. I set for myself and how the "Use-Modify-Create" (UMC) approach has played a key role in achieving them:

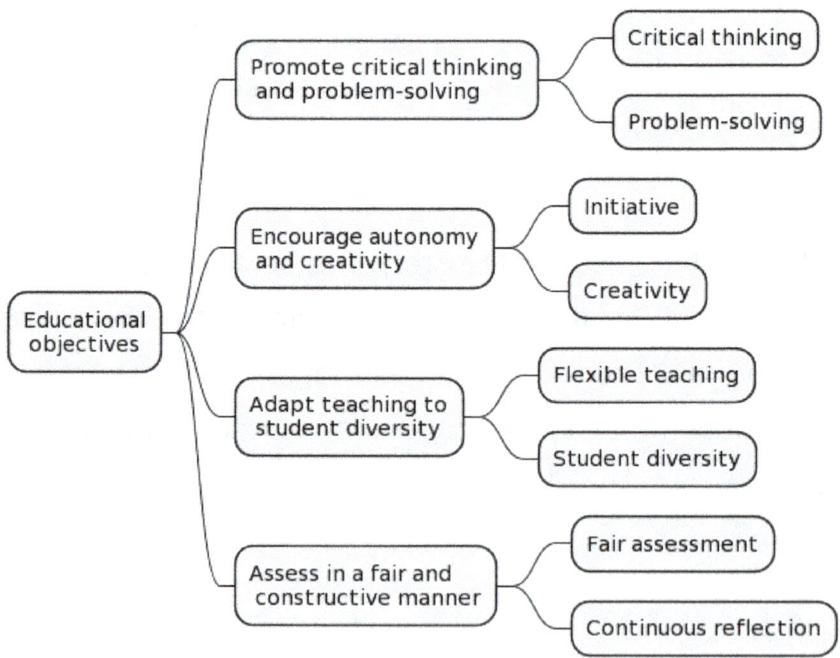

One of my main objectives has been to encourage students to develop critical thinking and problem-solving skills. The Use-Modify-Create (UMC) approach, with its progressive nature, has allowed students to immerse themselves in concrete problems, modify them, and ultimately create their own solutions, thus fostering analytical and innovative thinking.

**Promote critical thinking and problem-solving**

I have sought to create a space where students can take initiative, explore their ideas, and express their creativity. The "Create" phase of UMC has been particularly effective in this regard, offering students the freedom to design and execute their own projects, thereby strengthening their confidence and autonomy.

**Encourage autonomy and creativity**

Faced with the heterogeneity of skills in the classroom, I have aspired to develop differentiated teaching strategies. UMC, with its various phases, has provided a flexible structure that allows for adjusting the level of difficulty and support according to the individual needs of the students.

**Adapt teaching to the diversity of students**

**Assess in a fair and constructive manner**

The goal has also been to establish assessment methods that accurately reflect the skills and progress of the students. The Use-Modify-Create (UMC) approach has contributed to this goal by providing a clear framework for assessing students at each stage, while encouraging continuous reflection and improvement.

In summary, the "Use-Modify-Create" approach has been a valuable ally in achieving my educational objectives. It has offered a balanced and flexible structure, suited to the diversity of students and the changing demands of computer science, while promoting active, creative, and reflective learning.

# Why use the UMC approach?

Using the "Use-Modify-Create" (UMC) approach offers several advantages in teaching programming and computational thinking. Here are the reasons why it is beneficial to use it:

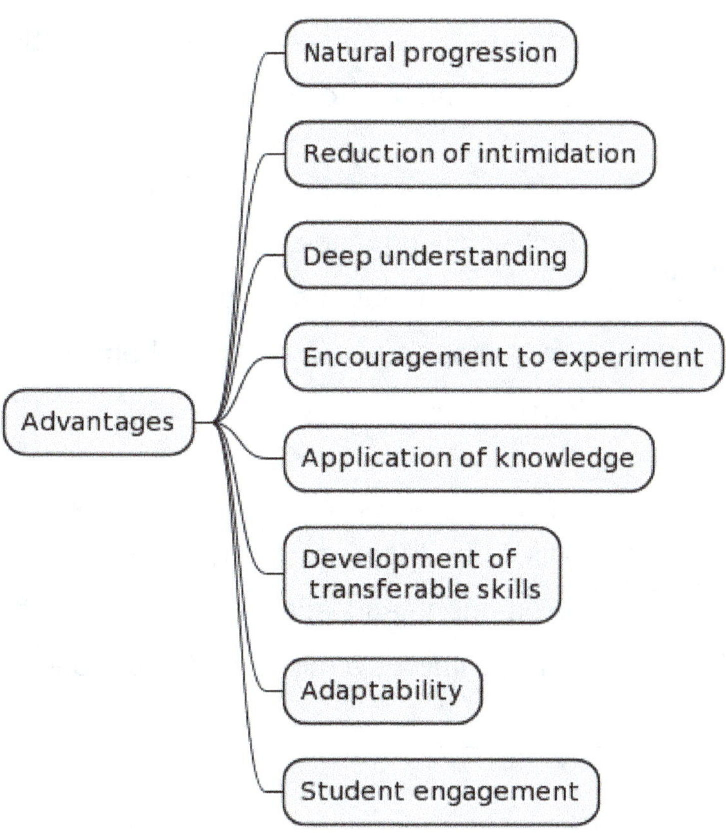

| | |
|---|---|
| **Natural progression** | The Use-Modify-Create (UMC) offers a natural progression of learning, from becoming familiar with a concept to mastering it completely. This allows students to build their skills step by step. |
| **Reduction of intimidation** | For beginners, creating code from scratch can be intimidating. Starting by using and modifying existing code helps students gain confidence before they embark on creating their own. |
| **Deep understanding** | By modifying code, students are encouraged to think critically about how it works. This enhances their understanding and enables them to identify and correct errors. |
| **Encouragement to experiment** | The modification stage encourages students to experiment and see how changes affect the outcome. This promotes a mindset of exploration and discovery. |

| | |
|---|---|
| **Application of knowledge** | The creation phase allows students to apply what they have learned in a practical context. This reinforces their understanding and demonstrates the relevance of the concepts studied. |
| **Development of transferable skills** | Beyond programming, the Use-Modify-Create (UMC) approach teaches skills such as problem-solving, critical thinking, and creativity, which are useful in many fields. |
| **Adaptability** | The UMC approach can be adapted to different age levels, skill sets, and content areas. Whether you are teaching children, adults, beginners, or advanced learners, UMC can be modified to meet the needs of the students. |
| **Student engagement** | By giving students the opportunity to modify and create, they become more invested in their learning. They see the value of what they are learning and are more likely to stay engaged. |

In conclusion, the "Use-Modify-Create" approach is an effective pedagogical tool that provides a clear structure for learning, while giving students the freedom to explore, experiment, and create. It promotes a deep understanding, builds confidence, and prepares students to apply their knowledge in real-world situations.

# Advantages and disadvantages

| Advantages | Disadvantages |
| --- | --- |
| Natural progression of learning | May be perceived as too structured for some students who prefer a more freeform approach |
| Reduces intimidation for beginners | |
| Reinforces deep understanding | Requires resources and pre-existing code examples for the "Use" and "Modify" phases |
| Encourages experimentation and discovery | |
| Practical application of knowledge | May not be suitable for all computer science subjects or concepts |
| Develops transferable skills | Students might rely too heavily on existing code and not explore on their own |
| Adaptable to different age and skill levels | |

It is important to note that the disadvantages mentioned largely depend on the implementation of the approach and how it is adapted to a particular group of students. In many cases, with proper planning and adaptation, these disadvantages can be minimized.

# Conclusion

## The future of UMC in computer science education

The pedagogical approach of UMC (Use – Modify - Create) in computer science education, particularly in Python programming, appears promising. This method, focused on intuitive understanding and adaptability, positions itself as a vehicle for innovation in the educational field. It offers a suitable response to the constant challenges posed by the rapid evolution of information technologies.

UMC, with its natural and inclusive approach, demystifies programming for a broader audience, ranging from students to professionals looking to change careers or improve their skills. This method could revolutionize the way computer science is taught, making learning more accessible, more engaging, and more in tune with individual needs.

## Encouraging a culture of continuous learning

One of the main strengths of UMC is its ability to encourage a culture of continuous learning. In a world where computer science skills are increasingly in demand, learning cannot be perceived as a process with a definitive end. Instead, it should be seen as a continuous journey, where curiosity and adaptability are major assets.

By integrating principles of active learning and focusing on deep understanding rather than memorization, UMC prepares learners to adapt to technological changes and to independently solve complex problems. This approach is essential for training not only competent programmers but also innovative thinkers and lifelong learners.

In conclusion, UMC is not only an effective teaching method for the Python language but also an adaptable educational model for various fields of computer science. Its future looks bright, promising to transform computer science education into a more enriching, dynamic, and 21st-century-aligned experience.

# Glossary

**"Trigger" activity**

A trigger activity is designed to spark students' interest, arouse their curiosity, and prepare them to approach a new topic or learning unit. It often serves as an introduction to a teaching sequence.

**Inductive pedagogical approach**

In this approach, learning begins with the observation or experimentation of concrete examples or real-life situations. From these observations, students deduce principles, rules, or theories. In other words, it starts from the specific to generalize.

**Pedagogical differentiation**

An approach to teaching that adapts content, process, and product based on students' interests, level of preparedness, and learning needs.

**Constructivism**

Constructivism is a learning theory that suggests individuals actively construct their own understanding and knowledge of the world through their experiences and by reflecting on these experiences.

| | |
|---|---|
| **Computational thinking** | A set of skills and mindsets that enable individuals to formulate problems and design solutions using computing. |
| **UMC (Use, Modify, Create)** | A three-step pedagogical approach for teaching programming and computational thinking. |

# By the same author

## Teaching Python Programming:

An innovative and practical approach

**Practical version**

*20 **Concrete** examples (Programming fundamentals, Control structures, Data collections, Advanced programming, Data structures and algorithms)*

## Les réseaux informatiques: Kit de survie

*Master IP addresses and computer networks in No Time!*

© Miguel DELAMONTAGNE